# PRAYERS OF LIFE

## John Birch

# DEDICATION

For the many who have offered encouragement.

# CONTENTS

Acknowledgments    i

1  Blessings    1

2  The day ahead    10

3  The journey of faith    25

4  Looking for guidance    48

5  People around us    52

6  In the world    67

7  Saying sorry    76

8  Saying thank you    80

9  When times are hard    83

10  Conflicts and disasters    97

The author    105

# ACKNOWLEDGMENTS

Thanks to the many who follow my daily postings on the Faith and Worship Facebook page, as this is this main source for the contents of this book, and the daily encouragement to take time out at the start of the day and concentrate on nothing more than a single prayer thought. It is an interesting discipline for one whose thoughts are normally very scattered and disorganized!

Some of these prayers were published in an eBook entitled 'Prayers for Today'

.

# 1 : BLESSINGS

God's love surround you
God's Word inspire you
God's strength sustain you
God's footsteps guide you
God's warmth enfold you
From morning till night

Bless the life that you live
Bless the peace that you bring
Bless the love that you give
Bless the song that you sing

God's peace
be in you,
God's love
enfold you,
God's word
direct you,
God's joy
uphold you,
God's strength
protect you,
today and always.

May your day be blessed
by moments of quietness,
light in your darkness,
strength in your weakness,
grace in your meekness,
joy in your gladness,
peace in your stillness.
May your day be blessed

God's strong arm protect you
God's firm feet support you
God's Holy Spirit surround you
God's gentle whisper calm you
in all life's storms and gales.

In your giving
and receiving,
your loving
and forgiving,
your going
and returning,
your working
and unwinding,
your growing
and maturing,
your living
and your dying,
God's blessing
surround you.

In your loving
and forgiving
may you be blessed.
In your giving
and receiving
may you be blessed.
in your trusting
and believing
may you be blessed,
this day and always.

Bless those who feed the poor
Bless those who heal the sick
Bless those who teach the young
Bless those who help the weak
Bless those who lend a hand
Bless those who share a tear
Bless those who walk beside
Bless those who give, not take

May God bless you
with a song in your heart,
a smile on your face
and a sparkle in your eyes,
for you are loved
and this world should know.

May the peace of God
be a resting place,
for souls to be still,
burdens laid down,
hands to reach up,
strength to be found.

The arms of God surround you
The mercy of God restore you
The word of God excite you
The love of God flow from you
The power of God sustain you
This day and all days, Amen.

God's light be in your eyes
God's word be in your mouth
God's breath be in your lungs
God's joy be in your heart
God's love be in your arms
God's strength be in your feet
Wherever God may lead you


May the grace of God
be seen in your eyes.
May the peace of God
be heard in your words.
May the love of God
be shown in your hands
May the joy of God
be sung in your heart.


God's peace surround us,
God's love inspire us,
God's grace transform us,
God's joy flow from us,
and bless this world through us.

The peace of God be in your heart
The grace of God be in your words
The love of God be in your hands
The joy of God be in your soul
and in the song that your life sings.


God's love surround you,
God's Spirit guide you,
God's whisper cheer you,
God's peace calm you,
God's shield protect you,
God's wisdom arm you,
wherever God may lead you.


May God's truth be in your words
May God's Love shine in your eyes
May God's peace infuse your days
May God's joy light up your heart

May God's Spirit surround you,
and those whom you love.
Rest now, in that calm embrace,
let your hearts be warmed
and all storms be stilled
by the whisper of his voice.


May peace flow
as a gentle stream
through your soul,
love's pure warmth
soften your heart,
and joy in the Lord
shine in your face
and all your words.


Blessing be on every hand
that does God's work.
Blessing be on every foot
that treads God's path.
Blessing be on every voice
that speaks God's word.
Blessing be on every heart
that seeks God's will.

God bless you on the journey
A light to show its many blessings
Strength to tread both hill and vale
Companionship with fellow travellers
Nourishment for each new day
A guide along the winding path
Somewhere you might safely rest
God bless you on the journey.


May the Light of God
be with you on your journey
May the Bread of life
sustain you on the road
May the Living Water
refresh your heart and soul
May the Good Shepherd
always lead you safely home.

## 2 : THE DAY AHEAD

Thank you for this day,
a gift gratefully received -
the opportunities within
waiting to be released;
the people I shall meet
and in your love embrace;
the challenges that come
and together we will face;
the service I can give
which is my thanks offering.

May your light
shine in our eyes.
May your voice
be in our words.
May your love
open our hearts.
May your joy
lighten our steps.
This and every day.

For this new day, we pray,
be in our conversations
and interactions with others,
that we might both show
and sow your love and grace
in our words and actions
with family, neighbours,
friends, and colleagues,
in our service, Lord, to you.

Forgive any reluctance
we might have to engage
fully with this new day.
Replace our detachment
with expectation,
for all we might achieve
if we put our trust in you
and your confidence in us.

This day reveal to you
the beauty in a smile
the wisdom of a child
the healing in a kiss
the joy of an embrace
the music of this world
the voices to be heard
the peace in being still.

As this day unfolds
and presents us
with its challenges,
may we face them
with confidence,
for you are with us
in our daily labor,
a constant help,
our strength and joy.

As we walk into this new day,
gracious God, help us focus
on our relationship with you
and all our fellow travelers,
always willing to be a guide
to those who are uncertain,
as they navigate this world,
of their ultimate destination.

Within the rushing around
and busyness of this day,
Lord, we pray for those
who simply pass us by -
shoppers, workers,
parents and toddlers,
teenagers, seniors,
unemployed, homeless -
strangers all to us
but precious in your eyes,
asking that you meet them
at their point of need
and bring into their lives
the wholeness they desire.

May this day become a blessing
through the people we meet,
conversations that take place,
opportunities we embrace,
challenges overcome,
and your presence with us
both to strengthen and inspire.

God be in you... always
God be in your resting
God be in your waking
God be in your busyness
God be in your quietness
God be in your speaking
God be in your listening
God be in your fullness
God be in your emptiness
God be in your laughing
God be in your weeping
God be in you... always.

For every pause
in this busy day -
time to stop,
time to listen,
time to see,
time to smile,
time to share,
time to pray,
time... to be,
we give you thanks.

Be our inspiration today,
as we walk your path,
speak your word,
offer our hands
and share your love
willingly, with all we meet.

Bring your peace
into our work;
the decisions
that we make,
conversations
taking place,
opportunities
to be grasped,
the stresses
we shall face.
And may it be
in our lives
that your peace
can be discerned.

May we daily be mindful
not only of others' needs
but those of ourselves,
taking time to be still,
rest from our busyness,
and in your embrace
breathe in your peace,
God of wholeness, we pray.

May we be a blessing today
to the many we shall meet -
on subway, foot or train,
in shopping mall, corner store,
busy supermarket aisle
or in the checkout queue,
in workplace and leisure space,
with friends or simply at home.
May we be a blessing today,
our smile contagious,
our words encouraging,
our attitude humble,
thinking only, if you were here,
what would you say or do?

For those who have no peace
within their daily schedules,
balancing needs of family
around hours of work,
struggling to find time
they can call their own,
bless them as they strive
to do the best they can
for those they love.
Grant them space
to breathe, relax, be still
within their busy lives,
the strength to carry on,
and the grateful support
of those at work and home.
May they know they are loved.

May you know the peace of God
May you show the love of God
May you feel the power of God
through the challenges of today.

May the words
I speak today
be uplifting.
May the love
I share today
be generous.
May the work
I do today
be productive.
May the life
I live today
be unselfish.
For your glory
and not mine, Lord.


May you begin this day
with the sure knowledge
that God is with you,
and when difficulties
and conflicts arise,
you will be able
to reflect His love,
peace and patience
in your response.
May your life each day
be a witness to your faith,
lived for the glory of God.

Your love be seen
in our greeting
and embracing,
in our thinking
and conversing,
in our giving
and receiving,
in our holding
and releasing,
in our winning
and our losing,
in our laughing
and our crying,
in our living
and our dying,
Your love be seen,
Your love be seen.

Bless this day,
this blank page
newly turned.
May its story,
once written,
bring only glory
to your name.

Creator God, by your transforming power
take the scattered stones of this day
and from them create something beautiful
that will bring glory to your name.

May you be found today,
in unexpected places
by unsuspecting people
going about their daily lives.
May you be found today,
in predictable places
by inquisitive people
searching for a different life.
May you be found today, Lord!

Know that God is,

wherever you are

Bless the people
behind the faces
I shall pass today -
the smiling faces,
thoughtful faces
downcast faces,
care-free, cared-for,
pampered, neglected,
smooth-skinned
and well-worn faces,
all telling their stories
of joy and sorrow,
laughter and pain.
Draw close to them,
these strangers,
part of your family,
and bless them today.


May the love of God
be in our eyes,
our hearts,
our words,
our hands,
and reach out
to touch the world.

Be our constant companion
through this coming week -
the one we can turn to
when others desert us,
pain starts to haunt us,
stress overwhelms us
and time is against us.
Be our constant companion,
our fellow traveler,
encourager, healer,
peace-bringer, power,
our heavenly Father.
Be our constant companion
on this day and all days. Amen

At the beginning of this day
bring your light and hope
into our hearts and souls,
that we may go out with joy
into a world that needs to see
your love shine through the dark,
and know there is much more
to life than they ever seen before.

May we embrace the challenges
that face us through this day
and, knowing you are with us
be filled with confidence and peace

Creator God, take the raw material
that is our lives, and from it make
something beautiful and useful today.

And at the end of the day...

As you are with us on this day's journeying
so embrace us through the evening hours,
our companion should we be lonely,
our strength when weary, peace if stressed,
encouragement through troubled times
and our comfort as we lay down to rest.

.

# 3 : THE JOURNEY OF FAITH

Grant us the grace to forgive,
to let go of the hurts
that we have carried,
and which now lay heavy
upon our hearts.
May we know the freedom
forgiveness can bring,
not only to perpetrator
but victim also,
and in that knowledge
find our hearts are set free.

May we never be afraid
of moving from our comfort zones
into new and unfamiliar places.
May we always be willing
to go wherever you might need us,
on this daily pilgrimage of faith.


Encourage us
in forgiveness,
practicing often
until it becomes
not simply easier
or less traumatic,
but who we are.


On the journey of faith be our guide,
a helping hand if the path is steep,
encouragement should our steps falter,
reassurance that beyond the clouds
the sun is shining and our destination
is more glorious than we can imagine.

Give us words that speak of love
Give us hands that work for peace
Give us feet that will not tire
Gives us hearts that show your grace.

Be still, my soul,
just for a moment,
be still, and know
the warm breeze
of God's Spirit
gently embracing.
Be still, and hear
the quiet words
of God's Spirit
gently uplifting.
Just for a moment,
just for a moment,
be still, my soul.

Christ Jesus, may we not be afraid
to overturn a few tables,
as you did within the temple,
when the need arises
for someone to speak up for Truth.

In this confused
and fragile world,
strengthen our faith,
increase our love,
and let your peace
flow through us,
that we might be
an ocean of calm
in what has become
a restless sea.

Cultivate your love within us
and encourage it to flower,
that its seed, scattered
by the breath of your Spirit,
might beautify this world.

Guide and protect us
along safe paths
through this world;
and if we stumble
along the way, eyes
and ears diverted
by sights and sounds,
or should we fall
and cry for help,
then hear our call,
and lift us once again,
as a parent would a child,
into your loving arms.
Guide and protect us,
Loving God, we pray.

Spirit of love, Spirit of peace,
pour through troubled hearts
as would a mountain stream
when winter turns to spring,
sweeping away the stones
that until now have impeded
your flow, and carrying them
into the ocean of your grace.


We thank you for all
who take on the role
of guide to travelers
journeying in faith.
Grant them wisdom,
patience, and strength
as they support those
who stumble and fall
upon this narrow path.
Bless both travelers
and those who guide,
that they may safely
reach their destination.

Bring completeness, Lord,
to those of us who are
still 'work in progress',
that we might glorify you
through our faith and lives.

May we see this world
with your eyes.
May we hear this world
with your ears.
May we teach this world
with your truth.
May we touch this world
with your peace.
May we heal this world
with your love.

For all whose journey
feels like wandering
through a wilderness,
guide them safely,
by day and night,
through desert places
into your promised land.

Your love surrounds us,
yet sometimes
we choose to be alone,
close the door,
leave you waiting,
patiently,
for the right time
to knock once more
and be let in.
A love that is gentle,
understanding
and yet persistent,
wanting to be known,
waiting to be embraced.
For such love, we thank you.

In times of uncertainty
it is good to know, Lord,
that whatever happens
we can depend on you,
a secure foundation
on which we have built
that no wind of change
can ever shake or damage.
And in that knowledge
we can endure all things,
for you are there, always,
a firm rock beneath our feet.

Unwrap the words
of Scripture for me,
that I might be fed
and faith built up
for my journeying,
each day, with you.

Grant us wisdom, Lord,
that we might answer
not only the questions
about our faith
that others ask of us,
but also those that lie
unanswered in our hearts
that, until this moment,
we have been afraid
to ask of you.

Be a soothing voice
within the storms
that often seem
to overwhelm us,
calming the waters
through which we sail,
stilling the winds
that would divert us,
guiding us safely
throughout this day.

Divine Potter, your work is never done,
continually remolding and shaping us
into the image of who we could be,
while this clay is willing to be changed.

Teach us your way, Lord,
when we are unsure
of which way to turn,
tiredness descends
and we're hurting inside.
Teach us your way, Lord,
when we are anxious
and struggle to pray,
unsure of the words
that we're wanting to say.
Teach us your way, Lord,
as we travel in faith
through uncertain times,
following your footsteps
with your word as our guide.
Teach us your way, Lord,
Teach us your way.

Quench the thirst we feel,
the dryness within
that this world's wisdom
can never satisfy.
Flow through these veins
until our hearts
are infused with your love
and our lives
filled to overflowing.

Lord, we would seek you
not only through revelation
and in tongues of fire,
but in the gentle whisper
that prompts us to action,
brings words to our mouths
and compassion in our hearts;
in love so beautifully expressed
through times of tragedy
as well as days of joy,
in power and in weakness,
in sacrificial service.
Lord, we would seek you.

Help us see this world
as through your eyes,
and this world see you
reflected through ours.


Gracious Lord, be our daily guide;
keep us on the path of Truth
and steer us away from
the loose stones of falsehood.


Heavenly Father
may our lives speak of you,
our hands work for you,
and the song in our heart
become a blessing to all who hear.

May we be peacemakers
in a world that would dull
our God-given senses
of sadness, grief and pain
through endless acts of
violence and terrorism.
May our lives and words
reveal a better way to live,
one that values everyone
and the sanctity of life.
May we be peacemakers
in this, our beautiful,
fragile, God-given world.

In our moments of melancholy,
loneliness and self-doubt,
bring to mind Scripture's words,
inscribed upon our hearts,
that you are with us always,
your presence bringing peace,
a healing balm in our distress.

Speak to us through your Word.
Speak to us through your world.
Speak to us through our friends.
Speak to us through our enemies.
Speak to us through sunny days.
Speak to us through storm and rain.
Speak to us through joyful times.
Speak to us through grief and pain.
Speak to us, make us listeners.
Speak to us, make us learners.
Speak to us, make us doers
so our lives can speak to others.

In a confusing world,
where truth is often
difficult to discern,
may it be your words
to which we turn.
Be our confidence
within uncertainty,
your words our peace,
your truth our reality.

Thank you, Jesus,
that you are there
when we stumble;
overly burdened,
carrying too much
upon our shoulders,
weary, seeking rest.
You take our load,
if we will let you,
and our weariness,
fashioning for us
your yoke instead,
a comfortable fit
to do your work
within this world.

Gracious God, open our eyes,
that may we never lose sight
of you, and attune our ears
so we can hear your gentle
but insistent whisper, each day
reminding us that we are loved,
as is the whole of your creation.

Grant us the humility to admit
that sometimes we are wrong,
don't always have the answer,
struggle through some days
while friends still think we're strong.
Grant us the humility to admit
our weakness and our need
when, distracted, we lose sight
of the One from whom
our strength and wisdom comes.

In the darkness of the night,
or the sun's revealing rays,
God is with us, always with us.
If the world be full of praise,
or we're hurt by what men say,
God is with us, always with us.
Should the way ahead be clear,
or a mist obscure our way,
God is with us, always with us,
God is with us every day.

Be the breath that wakes
our hearts from slumber,
be a wind that fills our sails.
Be the sun which guides
our journeys onward,
be a voice that stills the waves.


May we be followers
not of this world's
latest fashions,
consumer trends,
financial indexes
or lifestyle gurus,
but of a servant
who had no home
or worldly wealth,
yet through whom
the poor were rich
and the least of all
were daily blessed,
a divine paradox.
May we followers
of this servant King,
and through service
bring his blessing
to a world in need.

As I walk with you, Lord,
I begin to see this world
as you must do, and know
we must work together
to make it a better place,
which begins with hearts
hands and feet in service.

We give thanks for those
who, by their words
in books, street or pulpit,
were a necessary spark
igniting the kindling
you had so carefully
placed within our hearts,
the warmth from which
we still remember
with gratitude and praise.

John Birch

Your Word -
the steps we climb
that lead us
to a higher place,
a mountain top
from where
we see this world
and ourselves
from your perspective,
and stand in awe
and wonder.

What a joy it is
to know that we
are not only
son, daughter,
brother, sister,
but together, family,
with a heavenly Father
who knows us well,
cares for us,
laughs with us,
often weeps for us,
yet loves us still.

Within each day may there be
peace within my busyness,
space where I can rest awhile,
and listen to your gentle voice
before engaging with the world.

In our reading of Scripture
may we allow sufficient time
for its words to leave the page,
find their way into our hearts
and become a daily blessing
within family, work and leisure.

May we never be afraid
to admit we're struggling,
and reach out and grasp
your hand *before* we fall.

In your presence, Lord,
we offer all we have -
our loaves and fish-
that in your hands
they may be used
and multiplied,
our faith increase,
and other lives
be fed and satisfied.


You are
the life
I live,
the joy
I share,
the peace
I bring,
the love
I show,
the prayer
I pray,
the song
I sing.

Your Word is light
shining in our eyes.
Your Word is truth
among so many lies.
Your Word is peace
within a troubled soul.
Your Word is life
making the broken whole.


Lord, help us see
through your eyes
the potential
locked within us
simply waiting
to be released,
so we may become
the people you see.
Grant us courage
to open our hearts
and accept the key.

# 4 : LOOKING FOR GUIDANCE

When the question is 'Why?'
be the voice that I hear
When the question is 'Where?"
be the guidance I need
When the question is 'When?
Be the wisdom I seek
When the question is 'How?'
be the strength I require
When my answer is 'Yes!'
be the peace that I feel.

Lord, dispel the mists ahead
so we may more easily discern
this path you ask us to follow,
to the places you want us to be.


Be the light
we follow
Be the truth
we affirm
Be the life
we live by
Be the strength
we require


If the way ahead is obscured
by the mist of our uncertainties,
clear our minds and vision
that we might, once more,
have confidence to follow
the path along which you lead us.

Within the busyness
of our work and play
may we be aware
of the possibility
of your prompting,
keeping ears attuned
for your gentle whisper
breaking through,
bringing wisdom,
guidance, peace,
enriching our daily lives.


For those struggling
through stormy seas,
growing weary
of the journeying
and losing sight
of their destination,
be the lighthouse
that guides them
past hidden dangers,
into calmer water
and the safe harbor
of your loving arms.

You call, and so often,
amid the bustle of our day,
we're distracted
and fail to hear your voice.
You knock, but our lives
are untidy, unprepared,
and so we pretend
we never heard the sound.
Forgive us, Lord,
who look to you for guidance,
but only on our terms,
- when we call you -
and so often your need of us
is in the 'now' of our busy-ness,
which can be 'inconvenient'.
Forgive us, Lord,
may the door of our hearts
be open, and our ears attuned
for that unexpected call.


In the mist of doubt
be the word we hear
and the light we see.

# 5 : PEOPLE AROUND US

Gracious God, reach out,
to those who are lonely,
to the frail and elderly,
the young and vulnerable,
the poor and friendless,
the lost and forsaken;
and where necessary,
use these hands and arms
as if they were your own.

Lord, we celebrate
the differences
between us;
all that defines us,
our uniqueness,
who we are
in our eyes and yours.

Bless the many people
to whom we entrust
the care of our children;
the baby sitters, childminders,
nursery workers, teachers,
doctors, nurses, grandparents,
aunts, uncles and neighbors
who together will become
part of an extended family
bringing love and laughter
into the lives of both
parent and child.
Bless their contribution
and the care that they give.

Remind us often, Lord,
of your words, when some
would tell us otherwise,
that we have neighbors
in this world of ours
who are your children,
living in makeshift tents,
refugee camps, prisons,
subways, shop doorways -
neighbors who are hungry,
desperate, ignored, in need
of the very basics of life,
a new beginning, a chance
of calling somewhere home.
(Matthew 25:34-40)

Your love for humankind
extends far beyond
the barriers we create
at country borders
and within our minds.
Oh, that ours might also, Lord.

Break down the barriers
that we have erected;
the political, cultural,
sexual and religious
intolerances that divide,
rather than enhance us
as a civilized people,
and from the rubble
help us create a world
that is more tolerant
of difference, more willing
to embrace the stranger
and less interested in self.
As always, Lord, begin with me.

Bless the place that we call home,
be it mansion or tenement,
makeshift or permanent,
a thing of beauty -
or an embarrassment.
Bless the people within -
old, young, middle-aged.
Bless the conversation within -
love shared, prayers prayed.
Wherever, whatever it might be
bless the place that we call home.

Help us to share, honestly,
the faith that we hold dear -
the knowledge of your presence
both in worship and in pain,
prayers that have been answered
and those that still remain,
following your footsteps
through the sunshine and the rain.
Help us to share, honestly,
the faith that we hold dear.

Be with our children, Lord,
growing up into a fragile world.
Help them in the choices
and decisions that they face,
steer them away from harm.
If they have yet to follow you,
be there when they get lost
and be their guiding light.
Be with our children, Lord,
and together, with your help,
may this become a better,
safer and more equal world
for their offspring to inhabit.

Protect the vulnerable
who are so easily led astray
and, in craving acceptance
find it difficult to say no,
for fear of losing face.
May they know your love
which makes no demands,
accepts each one as equal,
and leads them, not astray,
but to a far safer place
within your loving arms.

Good Shepherd, we pray
for the homeless -
the misfits, rejected,
damaged, hungry,
hope-less people -
struggling to survive
not far from where we live.
Bless those who care,
who feed and clothe
and offer companionship
to these forgotten people,
and may we play our part,
rather than cross the road
or look the other way.

Help us to help those
who are struggling
through this day.
Neighbor, relative,
stranger or friend,
where we see a need,
rather than walk away
may we stop awhile
and share a hand,
a listening ear,
a smile, a prayer,
compassion, love,
just as you would do.


For the miracle of birth,
new life entering this
beautiful but fragile world
in innocence and love
we give you thanks.
For the joy of parenthood,
and the potential
to be nurtured lovingly
within that tiny child,
we give you thanks.
Bless them all, we pray.

Give strength to those
who cannot start this day
without the help of others,
and where simple tasks
we face are mountains
that must be climbed.
Equip those who care,
professionals and family,
with the skills required,
and the necessary gifts
of patience and love,
that each day's burden
might become lighter
and both be blessed.

Bless all who care for children,
growing up into a world
that seems more fragile
than it did a generation ago.
Bless them with the gifts of love,
joy, peace, patience and truth,
that, sown as seeds in childhood,
might germinate and grow,
becoming fruitful as the years go by,
when they have children of their own.

We pray for families
with almost enough,
but not quite
enough, for this week,
next week, every week;
slipping, then tumbling
further into debt.
Bless those who help
with practical advice,
compassion, giving, love;
and help us to help those
who are our neighbors
in your eyes, if not yet ours.


Bless those for whom this day
is one more mountain to be climbed,
and even rising from their bed
is the first of many obstacles
that must be overcome.
Healing God, equip them,
strengthen muscle, nerve and bone.
May this mountain be lower
than at first it seemed,
so they might stand upon its peak
and be proud of their success,
before returning safely to their homes.

Gracious God, bless those who,
because of increasing years
are struggling with daily tasks
that would, not long ago,
have been accomplished
in just a fraction of the time,
and without increasing pain.
Bring healing and comfort
to aching joints and muscles,
and ease their frustration
at this slowing down of life.
Bless them, and use their gifts,
knowledge and wisdom
that younger lives might
be touched and blessed
by these, your older children.


Bless those who are alone,
through circumstance or choice,
and bring them companionship,
if not through human contact
then through your closeness,
the knowledge of your presence
inhabiting their solitude,
filling their emptiness with peace.

Bless our children, Lord,
growing up into a future
that is difficult to predict.
Protect them, guide them
and give them wisdom
to see above and beyond
the tempting choices
this world may offer,
that they might become
the people who, in your eyes,
they were always meant to be.


Let us never forget,
in our haste to
discriminate,
that your blood
was shed for all,
not just a chosen few
defined by colour
race or creed,
that all might be saved
and know the joy
of belonging
within your family.

Lead us, gracious Lord,
to those who seek,
who have a hunger
and thirst for Truth,
but have yet to find you,
that we might share
from the abundance
that we have received;
mercy, forgiveness,
love without measure,
peace in our heart.
And in that encounter
may souls be fed
and thirst satisfied.

We pray for all those
exploring new beginnings
in employment or study,
and seeking your will
at this stage in their lives.
As they step out in faith
on this exciting journey
of discovery, be with them,
grant confidence and peace,
that they might become
the people you want them to be.

Bless the struggling,
for whom this day,
like many others,
is a mountain
yet to be climbed.
Be there for them,
a guiding hand
on stony ground,
help to carry
the load they bear,
encouragement
along the way.
And, where needed,
may your hands
and voice be ours.


Be with those whose bodies
do not allow them to be
as active as they would like,
where bones and muscles
are no longer as strong
as they once were, or pain
restricts their movement
making difficult simple tasks.
Bring comfort, healing,
relief from pain, and grant
peace that only you can give.

Enter, Lord,
into the silence
of the lonely,
into the fears
of the elderly,
into the worries
of the family,
into the anger
of the victim,
into the misery
of the homeless,
into the pain
of the sufferer,
and as you enter
bring comfort,
healing, peace.

May there always be space
within this day's busyness
for people to sit and think,
look around, contemplate,
consider a bigger picture
than the one before their eyes,
of a Creator and a Savior,
and the true worth of their lives.

Bless those whose vocation
is the nurture of children
who have additional needs.
Bless parents, carers, siblings
who sacrificially share their love.
Bless teachers and assistants
whose skills and patience
help reveal the potential
you have always known is there,
and bless those within the world
who can appreciate the gifts
within these, your precious children,
and offer them employment
and the life that they deserve.

Bless the givers
of time, resources,
patience and love,
who see a need
and offer help,
who are your hands
within this world.

# 6 : IN THE WORLD

May your light shine
brightly over this country,
and in its warm glow
dark clouds of anxiety
and division be scattered,
shadows of deceit exposed,
and in your brightness
may grace and peace,
like a gentle breeze
refresh our weary hearts.

May those who walk
or have been led
into the dark
open their eyes
and let your light
reveal the beauty
of true love and grace.

We remember, Lord,
the many families
struggling to survive
where rain and crops
have both failed,
leaving them without
food and clean water,
desperate and starving.
As we turn on our taps
and sit down to eat
we pray for them, Lord,
and for generosity
from those who have,
to those who have not,
in this, their hour of need.

The greatest love
is not to be found
in extravagant gestures
or gift-wrapped pleasures
that by their very nature
are often temporary,
but in the ordinariness
of a warm embrace,
a baby's cry, a mother's kiss,
heaven touching earth
as the world passed by.
That greatest love
can still be found
in the humblest places,
shine in many faces,
and be revealed
within the ordinariness
of simple gestures,
for in our willingness
to reach out, embrace,
heaven still reaches down
to touch the earth.

May the seed I sow today
through word and action,
be in soil you have prepared,
that will, in due season,
and fed by your Spirit,
produce a fruitful harvest.

As each morning's news reminds us,
we live in a fragile, uneasy world,
where truth and trust do not sit
comfortably together, and violence
instead of dialogue becomes the way
to end an argument or dispute.
Gracious God, may your love be seen
and your truth proclaimed
through the many lives and voices
of your children, and in its brightness
may those who now walk in shadows
choose to move into your light,
and embrace your mercy, love and peace.

Lord, bless the worldwide Church
which, though seemingly divided
by emphasis, liturgy and ritual
is still in your eyes family,
brothers and sisters united
by so much more than that
which keeps us apart,
a shared experience of grace
and love, amazing and divine,
and a common purpose, to bring
those who are still searching
to a place where you can be found.

Open our eyes
to the slavery
that still exists
in this world,
thinking less
about the price
that we pay,
thinking more
about the cost
in human life
and misery.

Ever-present God, be in
the ordinary moments
of this day; the cleaning
the house, feeding kids,
washing clothes, driving
to work, walking the dog,
on our own, in a crowd,
drinking tea, demanding
and unwinding moments.
Be the song that we sing
in our busyness and rest,
the ever-present friend
on whom we can depend.

Whenever hatred
endangers
all that we hold dear,
may love be
the weapon of choice
that we use,
and your light triumph
in the dark.

May our lives and voices
be a living testament
throughout this week,
reminding a world
grown tired of falsehood
that there is GOOD NEWS!

We pray for an end
to enslavement
in its many guises,
in this country
and further afield.
Open our eyes
to the situation.
Open our mouths
and raise our voices
in condemnation.
We pray for freedom.
We pray for justice
to be seen and done.

Gracious God, we bring to you
the marginalized, the struggling,
the working poor and unemployed,
waking up and wondering
how they are going to get through
this day and many more to come.
May we become part of the answer
to this prayer, a compassionate
and generous people, working
for the common good of all,
and seeing all as neighbors,
not simply strangers to ignore.
May we become a little more like you.


Bring peace, Lord,
into the vocabulary
of those in power;
and with it, patience,
kindness, goodness,
tolerance and love,
that we might discern
the precious fruit
of lives committed
to the common good
rather than self,
and this world become
a safer place to live.

Embrace this world,
it is a fragile place
in need of healing,
where arrogance
and self-interest
seek to undermine
your common good,
and those in need
take second place
to those who have.
Embrace this world,
wash it in your tears
of mercy and love,
and bring healing
and restoration
into its brokenness
dear Lord, we pray.

Let our voices be heard, Lord,
as we cry out against injustice,
unfairness, corruption,
exploitation and prejudice
as we follow your example
and, metaphorically at least,
overturn just a few tables
within this world's temple.
Let our voices be heard, Lord,

# 7 : SAYING SORRY

Forgive us, Lord,
for careless words
tossed out like stones,
that bruise and hurt.
Forgive us, Lord,
for careless thoughts
that lead to deeds
we then regret.
Forgive us, Lord,
when we forget
to live the life
we talk about.

If we should begin this day
thinking only of ourselves
and our personal concerns,
then forgive us, gracious God.
Open our hearts to embrace
the bigger world, the faces
both familiar and unknown
whose paths will cross with ours,
in subway, street or place of work;
and knowing of your care for them
may our greeting, helpful hand,
or simple act of courtesy
bring a spark of your love
into busy, often stress-filled lives.

Forgive us those times
when by action or word
we have failed to reflect
the faith that we profess,
and grant us a humility
that can swallow pride,
embrace those we've hurt,
and learn to apologize.

Grant us the humility
to express sorrow
whenever our words
or actions cause pain.
Grant us the humility
to show forgiveness
when our lives are hurt,
so that love wins the day.
And may that balance
in every relationship
bring glory to your name.

You have tasked us
with living and breathing
your Word, that others
might hear us speak of you
and see your light within.
Yet we still breathe in
this world's stale air
and are tempted by its ways.
Forgive us, strengthen us,
enable us to be the people
you know that we can be,
and your name be glorified
through our lives today.

Forgive us for believing
that in our own strength
and by our own wisdom
all things are possible,
and reveal to us instead
what you would have us do
and equip us for the task.

Loving God, forgive us
when we, too quickly,
choose the easy
and convenient path
which suits our daily life.
Increase our courage
to step out beyond
the comfortable
and familiar spaces
where we feel safe,
and follow you instead
to unfamiliar places,
where we can engage
more fully with a world
you love enough to die for.

# 8 : SAYING THANK YOU

Thank you, for a love
that is dependable,
not buffeted by wind
or wave, but constant
in its warm embrace.
Thank you, for a love
that is available,
not limited by time
or place, but offered
as your gift of grace.

Thank you for those
whose lives touch ours
and leave your mark

Creator God, thank you
for the beauty of sunrise,
as the darkness of night
is so gracefully swept away,
and in the sun's warm glow
we are reminded
that your love overcomes
life's darker moments,
lightens our journeying,
and in its warmth, embraces us.

Thank you for the knowledge
that, undeserving as we are,
you have faith in our ability
to be your hands and voices
here in this place, empowered
by your Spirit, encouraged
by your Word and motivated
by the needs of this fragile world.

For love beyond imaging,
that accepts us as we are,
and from such raw and
unpromising material
creates something new
and beautiful to use,
we thank you, gracious God.

For those who weave
from notes and scales
a graceful melody.
For those who see
within the stone
a face to be revealed.
For those who write
and in their words
transport us far away.
For the gift of creativity
we thank you, Creator God!

Thank you for the smile
that cheers us
Thank you for the hug
that warms us
Thank you for the song
that moves us
Thank you for the poem
that lifts us
Thank you for the word
that stirs us
Thank you for the hand
that helps us
Thank you for the feet
that guide us
Thank you for the love
that's shown us.

# 9 : WHEN TIMES ARE HARD

Where memory is failing,
and everyday tasks
become daily challenges
that tire and frustrate,
bring comfort, peace,
and the help of others.
Be the precious memory
that remains as others
gradually slip away,
of a love that is dear,
arms that embrace,
a shoulder to lean on
and a safe place to rest.

God of wholeness
be with the broken,
in body and mind;
be with the wounded
in spirit and soul;
bring restoration,
healing and peace.

Life is a precious gift,
a thing of beauty,
to be treasured,
not damaged
or destroyed.
Where hearts,
minds and bodies
are broken,
your gift abused,
pour out your love;
and forgive us,
when we forget
the value of this gift
of life, and our duty
of care to one another.

For We pray for those for whom
winter is a challenging time of year,
as shorter days and long dark nights
make it a struggle to socialize,
walk to the local shops or church,
and loneliness becomes a problem
that is difficult to overcome.
Bring light into their lives, Lord,
along with warmth and sustenance,
through the generosity of others,
the blessing of good health
and your presence by their side.

Help us overcome
our fears and doubts,
all that comes between
the things you ask of us,
and all that we believe
we are capable of.
Break down the barriers
that daily we create,
and enable us to become
all  that you ask us to be.

May those facing hostility
for the faith they profess
know you are with them,
understanding the fear
and hurt they endure.
Grant strength and hope.
May the love they share
and the forgiveness
they show break down
the barriers that divide
and tear communities apart.
May your victory on the Cross
be reflected in their lives,
and love triumph over hate.

Help us to forgive,
that you might lift
the heavy burden
we have carried
on our shoulders
for far too long,
and in its place
know the freedom
only you can give.

For those whose day
is tinged with sadness,
for lives that have gone
or love that's been lost,
bring moments of joy
in the remembering,
release from burdens
they need not carry,
and in this freedom
let them find peace
for their tomorrows.

Bless those who search
and have yet to find.
Broaden their vision
to take in your horizon,
release the chains
that restrain them,
and attune their ears
to your gentle,
but insistent voice,
whispering their name.

Healing God, bring wholeness
to lives that are broken
by circumstance or illness.
Your Spirit strengthen,
your peace sustain,
your love refresh,
your arms enfold
your warmth revive
these, your fragile children,
Healing God, we pray.

For all those whose days
are fully occupied
with the task of caring
for young and old,
bless them with patience,
compassion and love.
May they find peace
within their busyness,
and moments of joy
to lift their spirits
when low or weary.
As they are a blessing
to those under their care,
may they too be blessed.

Lord, we pray for the disappeared;
the 'have you see this person?'
in newspaper and social media
who is also son, daughter,
brother, sister, mother, father,
last seen somewhere and then,
missing, presumed lost or worse.
Guard and guide those who choose
this path, for whatever reason,
and if it be right then lead them
safely back into their homes.
And for families who wait, in fear
and hope, for news of loved ones,
grant them strength each day
until their missing one is found.


Be close to those for whom
life's journeying is over
and now is time for rest,
in the company of friends
and loved ones from the past,
welcomed into your house
and to a room that is prepared,
all brokenness made whole
and a new life to embrace.

Gracious God, for all lives
slowed down by pain
in muscle, nerve or joints,
may the healing oil
of your Spirit flow
through their bodies
bringing healing and release.

For those coming to terms
with a health diagnosis
that will impact not only
on their own lives but also
those of family and friends,
be especially close today.
As they reassess each day
in the light of this bad news,
bring a blessing as they awake
in the little things that once
would have passed them by,
and in the help and support
of loved ones, the doctors,
and all involved in their care.

May those who feel
grief's emptiness,
with words unsaid,
things left undone,
be freed from guilt
and know instead
your love's embrace,
and live in peace.

Give strength to those
who have grown weary,
doubtful or disillusioned
along the road of faith,
now wanting to rest awhile
or take a different route.
Open their eyes again
as with those two disciples
on the Emmaus road.
Let them hear your word,
feel your gentle touch
and know that it is you
still walking by their side.
Resurrect their faith,
bring to them new life,
living God, we pray.

Bring your soothing touch
to the aching joints
and muscles that once
could run for you
but move more slowly now,
and in our walking
if we should rest awhile,
reveal to us anew
the beauty in this world
that rushing, we once missed.

We pray for those for whom
this morning is a mountain
they are forced to climb,
because of circumstances
over which they have no control.
Help them in their distress,
hear their fears and cries.
Circle them, Lord, with your love;
in their weakness bring strength,
in their sorrow, moments of joy.
May their journey become easier
in your company, we pray.

Embrace in your loving arms
all who are grieving the loss
of family and loved ones
through tragic circumstance;
where lives are in turmoil,
hope turns to despair
and pain is all that's felt.
Be with them in their sorrow,
uphold them with your strength,
and through the generosity
of love shown by others
and your presence within their hearts
may they know they are not alone,
in their struggle through today.

Gracious God, be with all those
struggling today with symptoms
of dementia in its many forms;
mood changes, memory lapses,
confusion and helplessness.
May they know in their hearts
your comforting embrace
amid their daily frustrations,
and continue to realize,
as names and memories fade,
that they are still loved by family,
friends, and especially by you.

Healing God, bring wholeness
into lives broken by pain,
anxiety, hurt and anguish.
Enfold them in your arms.
May they sense your love,
and in that warm embrace
feel the Spirit's gentle flow
through muscle, joints,
veins, nerves and soul,
renewing, restoring,
enabling and freeing them
from the shackles of their distress.
Break those chains Lord, we pray.

When in the midst of illness
or infirmity fear takes over,
and faith takes second place
to the concerns of each hour,
be so close that we can feel
your Spirit's breath, and
the warmth of your embrace.
May we know your peace,
as you bring wholeness
into these, our fragile lives.

Bless those who struggle
to face each new day
with any sense of joy,
for whom the challenge
is feeding the family,
staying out of debt
and facing stark choices
that I am thankful
I do not have to make.
Bless those who help,
guiding and navigating
life's troubled waters,
and those whose gifts
of food and drink will,
if only temporarily,
keep this family afloat.


Bring light to those
who live in darkness.
and warmth to all
whose faith is cold.
Give bread to those
who daily hunger,
and living water
to all who thirst.

For all who struggle
day by day
to feed the family,
pay the bills,
keep warm at night,
treat the kids,
find enough work,
enjoy life,
Lord, be with them,
and with us,
your hands and feet
in this world,
as we help them,
our neighbors
as best as we are able.


For all those times
when our shoulders
are not broad enough
for everything we carry,
and yet we still refuse
your hands held out,
grant us the humility
to recognize our limits,
embrace your strength,
and allow you to lighten
these heavy loads.

# 10 : CONFLICTS AND DISASTERS

As your Spirit once hovered
over the waters of a dark earth
bringing light and life
into a glorious new day,
so spread that same brightness
once more over this earth,
into the shadows of hearts
and stubbornness of minds
that see no further than self
and have no regard for life.
Bring light into our darkness,
a new dawn within our hearts,
Creator God, we pray.

May violence and hatred
never triumph over love,
and we who are witnesses
through newsfeed or TV
never take refuge in silence,
but speak and live loud
the faith that we profess,
and show the difference
even in our small world
that a little love can make.


For the displaced,
dispossessed,
throwaway
people,
refugees
forced to flee,
empty-handed,
homeless, hungry,
Loving God, we pray -
that generosity,
compassion,
food and love
be given to these,
your precious children,
in this, their time of need.

Loving God, we do not know
why anyone should feel
they have a given right,
through senseless violence,
to end the lives of others
and sow such grief and pain.
But of this we are certain,
it does not come from you.
Be close to all who grieve,
ease the suffering of those
affected by such atrocities,
and through love shown
and sown through communities,
bring an increasing measure
of healing and release.


Be with the forgotten people,
forced from their homes
for so many reasons,
living now on foreign soil
in temporary shelters,
reliant on charitable giving
for food to eat, warmth, life.
Merciful God, bring an end
to their suffering and distress.
May their children grow up
knowing where they belong,
and this world show them
the difference love can bring.

God of love, be with those
who live in constant fear,
not knowing when or where
the next bomb may fall,
or if this day is to be their last;
who struggle to find food
and water amidst the rubble
of a place called home
and live among the dead.
May these precious people
know their cries are heard,
that this world does care,
and be released from the pain
and suffering that is,
until now, their daily bread.

Pour your love,
as a flowing stream
of life-giving water
over a fragile world,
grown dry and weak,
and satisfy its thirst.

Be with the forgotten ones, Lord,
who were once  front page stories
but now are yesterday's news -
the millions starving in Yemen,
the one in 113 people on earth
now classed as refugees,
the enslaved, the trafficked,
the child soldiers, the abducted,
those caught up in endless wars,
while TV stations look elsewhere
for lighter, more uplifting news.
Be with the forgotten ones, Lord,
and stir the consciences of those
who could, through rank or influence
make a difference to these lives.


Loving God, raise up peace-talkers
peace-doers and peace-makers,
who are not afraid to speak out
against this world's injustices,
but above all else want an end
to bloodshed and destruction,
and see peaceful resolution, fueled
by your love and grace, replacing
the harmful rhetoric that leads to war.

When hatred is revealed
and its banner unfurled,
words turn to violence,
and innocent lives lost
in the name of race,
religion or political creed,
may your light be seen,
your voice be heard,
and this truth ring out,
that in the eyes of God
there is no place for hate
in a world made in love.
May your justice prevail,
your love triumph always,
gracious God, we pray.

Bless the doctors, nurses,
and all those risk-takers
prepared to step beyond
the safety of their normal lives
to help others in war zones,
refugee camps, and wherever
there is need, bringing wholeness
to bodies broken by conflict,
comfort to those in their care.
Keep them safe, bless their work
and all whose lives they touch.

Lord, have mercy
on all who have been persuaded
that violence and destruction
are the will of God,
and would sacrifice themselves
and the lives of others
for this perverse ideology.
Lord, have mercy.

For all those who, today,
are risking their lives
making hazardous journeys
across deserts and oceans
to escape persecution,
poverty and hunger
and seek a better life;
protect them from those
profiting from their situation,
selling dreams as flimsy
as the boats they put them on,
with absolutely no regard for life.
Keep them safe, but also
help politicians, agencies,
and policy makers trying
find a solution to what is
a growing humanitarian tragedy.

From our safe, cozy,
and familiar world
it is not easy,
and uncomfortable,
to picture refugees
fleeing conflict,
malnourished, thirsty,
dying of cholera
for lack of medical care,
while our world,
our comfortable world,
averts its gaze
or simply passes by.
Forgive us, Lord,
who let this happen
through our inaction.
For those in Yemen
and many other places,
bring comfort, aid, release
from fear and conflict,
and the life that they deserve.

# ABOUT THE AUTHOR

John Birch is a Methodist Local Preacher and writer living in South Wales, and has a website www.faithandworship.com which is a well-used resource of prayer and Bible study material.

Also available in paperback is *The Act of Prayer*, a collection of 700 lectionary-themed prayers, *Ripples – engaging with the world in prayer* and *Fragrant Offering*, a Celtic-inspired Liturgy.

Follow the author on his Faith and Worship Facebook page where new prayers are shared throughout the week.

John Birch

42932212R00068

Printed in Poland
by Amazon Fulfillment
Poland Sp. z o.o., Wrocław